CLEAN EATING

COOKBOOK

FOR

BEGINNERS

CLEAN EATING MADE EASY: EASY RECIPES FOR A HEALTHIER YOU

Table of Contents

Introduction

Welcome to the Clean Eating Cookbook for Beginners! If you're reading this, chances are you're ready to make a positive change in your life—one meal at a time. Clean eating isn't a fad diet or a quick fix; it's a lifestyle that focuses on nourishing your body with whole, natural foods while minimizing processed ingredients. The goal is simple: eat real food, feel better, and enjoy meals that are both delicious and satisfying.

Starting a clean eating journey can feel overwhelming at first. Grocery aisles are filled with processed options, packaged snacks, and foods with long ingredient lists that are hard to pronounce. This cookbook is designed to make the transition easy and enjoyable. With simple, beginner-friendly recipes, practical tips, and approachable meal ideas, you'll learn that clean eating doesn't have to be complicated or boring.

Inside, you'll find recipes for breakfast, lunch, dinner, and snacks—all made with wholesome ingredients that support energy, weight management, and overall health. You'll also discover tips for meal prep, pantry essentials, and ways to make your meals flavorful without relying on artificial additives. Whether you're cooking for yourself, your family, or both, these recipes are designed to be easy, nourishing, and, most importantly, delicious.

Clean eating is about more than just food—it's about creating a lifestyle that fuels your body and mind. By choosing fresh fruits and vegetables, lean proteins, whole grains, and healthy fats, you're giving yourself the tools to feel your best every day. Over time, you'll notice improvements in energy, mood, digestion, and even sleep.

This cookbook is your guide to starting small, building healthy habits, and enjoying the process. Remember: clean eating is a journey, not a destination. Celebrate your successes, experiment with flavors, and make each meal a step toward a healthier, happier you. Let's get started on this delicious journey to better health!

Tips & Tricks for Clean Eating Success

Starting a clean eating lifestyle can feel challenging at first, but with a few simple strategies, it becomes easy, enjoyable, and sustainable. Here are some practical tips and tricks to help you succeed on your journey:

1. Stock a Clean Pantry

Keep your kitchen stocked with whole, unprocessed foods like brown rice, quinoa, oats, nuts, seeds, canned beans, and natural spices. Having healthy staples on hand makes it easier to prepare meals without relying on processed options.

2. Plan Your Meals

Take a few minutes each week to plan breakfasts, lunches, dinners, and snacks. Meal planning reduces stress, prevents last-minute unhealthy choices, and helps you stick to your goals.

3. Cook in Batches

Prepare large portions of grains, proteins, or roasted vegetables and store them in the fridge or freezer. This saves time during busy days and ensures you always have healthy options ready.

4. Read Labels Carefully

Look for ingredients you can pronounce and avoid foods with added sugars, artificial flavors, or preservatives. Focus on whole, minimally processed foods as much as possible.

5. Embrace Fresh Produce

Fill half your plate with colorful fruits and vegetables. Fresh produce provides essential vitamins, minerals, and fiber while keeping meals satisfying and nutrient-dense.

6. Get Creative with Flavors

Use herbs, spices, citrus, and healthy oils to add flavor without relying on processed sauces or excessive salt. Experimenting with seasonings keeps meals exciting and delicious.

7. Stay Hydrated

Drinking enough water supports digestion, energy, and overall health. Herbal teas or infused water can also make hydration more enjoyable.

8. Practice Mindful Eating

Slow down and savor your meals. Eating mindfully helps you recognize hunger cues, prevents overeating, and allows you to truly enjoy the flavors of clean, wholesome food.

9. Make Small, Sustainable Changes

Clean eating is a journey, not a sprint. Start by swapping one or two processed items for healthier alternatives and gradually build from there. Small changes lead to lasting habits.

10. Keep It Fun

Experiment with new recipes, try seasonal ingredients, and involve family members in cooking. Enjoying the process makes it easier to stick with clean eating long-term.

By incorporating these tips and tricks into your routine, you'll find that clean eating is not just achievable—it's enjoyable. Use this section as a guide to set yourself up for success and make nourishing your body a natural, rewarding part of your life.

Energizing Breakfasts

Overnight Chia Pudding with Berries

INGREDIENTS:

1 ½ CUPS UNSWEETENED ALMOND MILK (OR OTHER PLANT-BASED MILK)
½ CUP CHIA SEEDS
1–2 TABLESPOONS PURE MAPLE SYRUP OR RAW HONEY (OPTIONAL, TO TASTE)
1 TEASPOON PURE VANILLA EXTRACT
1 CUP MIXED FRESH BERRIES (BLUEBERRIES, RASPBERRIES, STRAWBERRIES, OR BLACKBERRIES)
2 TABLESPOONS UNSWEETENED SHREDDED COCONUT OR SLICED ALMONDS (OPTIONAL TOPPING)

INSTRUCTIONS:

In a medium bowl or jar, whisk together the almond milk, chia seeds, maple syrup (if using), and vanilla extract until well combined.

Cover and refrigerate for at least 4 hours or overnight. Stir once after the first 30 minutes to prevent clumping.

Before serving, stir the pudding to achieve a creamy consistency.

Divide into two bowls or jars, then top with fresh berries and optional toppings like coconut or almonds.

Clean Eating Tip

Use unsweetened plant-based milk and skip the added sweetener if you prefer a naturally low-sugar option. Fresh, seasonal berries provide natural sweetness and antioxidants.

 PREP TIME: **10 MIN**   CHILL TIME: **4 HOURS**   SERVINGS: **2**

Veggie-Packed Omelet

INGREDIENTS:

2 LARGE EGGS (OR 3 EGG WHITES + 1
WHOLE EGG FOR LIGHTER OPTION)
2 TABLESPOONS UNSWEETENED ALMOND
MILK (OR WATER)
¼ TEASPOON SEA SALT
⅛ TEASPOON BLACK PEPPER
1 TEASPOON OLIVE OIL OR AVOCADO OIL
¼ CUP DICED BELL PEPPERS (ANY COLOR)
¼ CUP CHOPPED SPINACH OR KALE
¼ CUP DICED MUSHROOMS
2 TABLESPOONS CHOPPED RED ONION
2 TABLESPOONS CHERRY TOMATOES,
HALVED
OPTIONAL TOPPINGS: FRESH HERBS
(PARSLEY, CHIVES), SLICED AVOCADO, OR A
SPRINKLE OF FETA

INSTRUCTIONS:

In a small bowl, whisk together the eggs, almond milk, salt, and
pepper until fluffy.
Heat the olive oil in a nonstick skillet over medium heat.
Add bell peppers, mushrooms, onion, and tomatoes. Sauté for 3–4
minutes, until softened. Add spinach and cook another 1 minute,
just until wilted.
Pour the egg mixture over the veggies. Tilt the pan gently so the
eggs spread evenly.
Cook without stirring for 2–3 minutes until the eggs begin to set.
Carefully lift one edge and fold the omelet in half.
Continue cooking for another 1–2 minutes until the omelet is
cooked through but still tender.
Slide onto a plate and garnish with herbs, avocado, or feta if
desired.
Clean Eating Tip
Use whatever vegetables you have on hand — zucchini, broccoli,
or asparagus work well too. More color means more nutrients!

 PREP TIME: **10 MIN**   COOK TIME: **10 MIN**   SERVINGS: **1**

Greek Yogurt Parfait with Homemade Granola

INGREDIENTS:

FOR THE GRANOLA (MAKES ABOUT 2 CUPS):
2 CUPS OLD-FASHIONED ROLLED OATS
½ CUP RAW NUTS OR SEEDS (ALMONDS, WALNUTS,
PUMPKIN SEEDS)
2 TABLESPOONS COCONUT OIL, MELTED
3 TABLESPOONS PURE MAPLE SYRUP OR RAW HONEY
1 TEASPOON PURE VANILLA EXTRACT
½ TEASPOON GROUND CINNAMON
PINCH OF SEA SALT
FOR THE PARFAIT:
2 CUPS PLAIN GREEK YOGURT (2% OR NONFAT)
1 CUP FRESH BERRIES (BLUEBERRIES, RASPBERRIES,
OR SLICED STRAWBERRIES)
½ CUP HOMEMADE GRANOLA
2 TEASPOONS RAW HONEY OR MAPLE SYRUP
(OPTIONAL DRIZZLE)

INSTRUCTIONS:

Make the granola:
Preheat oven to 325°F (160°C).
In a large bowl, mix oats, nuts/seeds, cinnamon, and salt. Stir in
melted coconut oil, maple syrup, and vanilla until everything is
coated.
Spread evenly on a parchment-lined baking sheet.
Bake for 20–25 minutes, stirring halfway, until golden brown. Let
cool completely to crisp up.
Assemble the parfaits:
Spoon ½ cup Greek yogurt into each serving glass or bowl.
Add a layer of fresh berries, then 2–3 tablespoons of granola.
Repeat layers, finishing with berries on top.
Drizzle with honey or maple syrup if desired.
Clean Eating Tip
Store leftover granola in an airtight jar for up to 2 weeks —
perfect for quick parfaits, smoothie bowls, or healthy snacking.

 PREP TIME: **10 MIN**   COOK TIME: **30 MIN**   SERVINGS: **2**

Avocado Toast on Whole Grain Bread

INGREDIENTS:

2 SLICES WHOLE GRAIN OR
SPROUTED GRAIN BREAD,
TOASTED
1 RIPE AVOCADO
1 TEASPOON FRESH LEMON OR
LIME JUICE
PINCH OF SEA SALT
PINCH OF BLACK PEPPER
OPTIONAL TOPPINGS: CHERRY
TOMATOES (HALVED), RADISH
SLICES, CUCUMBER RIBBONS,
SPROUTS, RED PEPPER FLAKES,
OR A DRIZZLE OF EXTRA VIRGIN
OLIVE OIL

INSTRUCTIONS:

Toast the bread slices until golden brown and crisp.
In a small bowl, mash the avocado with lemon or
lime juice, salt, and pepper until creamy but slightly
chunky.
Spread the avocado mixture evenly over the toasted
bread.
Add your choice of toppings for extra flavor and
nutrition.
Serve immediately.
Clean Eating Tip
Choose sprouted or seeded whole grain bread for
more fiber, protein, and nutrients. Keep toppings
colorful — the more variety, the better for your body.

 PREP TIME: **10 MIN**

 SERVINGS: 2

Banana Oat Pancakes

INGREDIENTS:

1 CUP ROLLED OATS
1 MEDIUM RIPE BANANA
2 LARGE EGGS
¼ CUP UNSWEETENED ALMOND MILK
(OR ANY MILK OF CHOICE)
1 TEASPOON PURE VANILLA EXTRACT
1 TEASPOON BAKING POWDER
½ TEASPOON GROUND CINNAMON
PINCH OF SEA SALT
COCONUT OIL OR AVOCADO OIL, FOR
COOKING
OPTIONAL TOPPINGS: FRESH BERRIES,
SLICED BANANA, NUT BUTTER, OR A
DRIZZLE OF PURE MAPLE SYRUP

INSTRUCTIONS:

Place oats in a blender and pulse until they become a fine flour.
Add banana, eggs, milk, vanilla, baking powder, cinnamon, and salt. Blend until smooth.
Heat a nonstick skillet or griddle over medium heat and lightly grease with coconut oil.
Pour ¼ cup of batter for each pancake onto the skillet.
Cook 2–3 minutes, until bubbles form on the surface. Flip and cook another 1–2 minutes until golden and cooked through.
Serve warm with your favorite clean toppings.
Clean Eating Tip
Make a double batch and freeze extras. Reheat in a toaster or skillet for a quick, nutrient-packed breakfast on busy mornings.

 PREP TIME: **5 MIN**   COOK TIME: **10 MIN**   2 SERVINGS (ABOUT 6 SMALL PANCAKES)

Smoothie Bowl with Nut Butter Drizzle

INGREDIENTS:

FOR THE SMOOTHIE BASE:
1 FROZEN BANANA
½ CUP FROZEN BERRIES (BLUEBERRIES, STRAWBERRIES, OR MIXED)
½ CUP UNSWEETENED ALMOND MILK (OR OTHER PLANT-BASED MILK)
½ CUP PLAIN GREEK YOGURT (OPTIONAL FOR ADDED PROTEIN)
FOR TOPPINGS:
2–3 TABLESPOONS GRANOLA (PREFERABLY HOMEMADE OR LOW-SUGAR)
¼ CUP FRESH FRUIT (BERRIES, KIWI SLICES, OR MANGO)
1 TEASPOON CHIA SEEDS OR HEMP HEARTS
1 TABLESPOON NATURAL NUT BUTTER (ALMOND, PEANUT, OR CASHEW), WARMED FOR EASY DRIZZLING

INSTRUCTIONS:

In a blender, combine frozen banana, frozen berries, almond milk, and Greek yogurt. Blend until thick and creamy, scraping down the sides if needed. The mixture should be thicker than a smoothie for drinking.
Pour the smoothie into a bowl.
Arrange toppings: sprinkle with granola, layer fresh fruit, and add chia or hemp seeds.
Drizzle warmed nut butter over the top before serving.
Clean Eating Tip
Use unsweetened nut butter with no added oils or sugars. The natural sweetness of the banana and fruit keeps this bowl both clean and satisfying.

 PREP TIME: **10 MIN**

 SERVINGS: **1**

Quinoa Breakfast Porridge with Cinnamon & Apple

INGREDIENTS:

½ CUP UNCOOKED QUINOA, RINSED
1 CUP UNSWEETENED ALMOND MILK
(OR OTHER MILK OF CHOICE)
½ CUP WATER
1 SMALL APPLE, DICED (PEELED IF
PREFERRED)
1 TEASPOON GROUND CINNAMON
1 TEASPOON PURE VANILLA EXTRACT
1–2 TEASPOONS PURE MAPLE SYRUP
OR RAW HONEY (OPTIONAL, TO TASTE)
PINCH OF SEA SALT
OPTIONAL TOPPINGS: EXTRA APPLE
SLICES, CHOPPED WALNUTS OR
ALMONDS, CHIA SEEDS, OR A DRIZZLE
OF NUT BUTTER

INSTRUCTIONS:

In a medium saucepan, combine quinoa, almond milk,
water, diced apple, cinnamon, and sea salt. Bring to a
gentle boil.
Reduce heat to low, cover, and simmer for 15–20 minutes,
stirring occasionally, until the quinoa is tender and most
liquid is absorbed.
Remove from heat and stir in vanilla extract and maple
syrup (if using).
Divide into two bowls and top with your favorite extras
such as nuts, seeds, or more apple slices.
Serve warm.
Clean Eating Tip
Cook a bigger batch of quinoa in advance and reheat with
a splash of almond milk throughout the week for a quick,
nourishing breakfast.

 PREP TIME: **10 MIN**   COOK TIME: **20 MIN**   SERV2**1**

Hard-Boiled Egg & Veggie Snack Box

INGREDIENTS:

4 LARGE EGGS
1 CUP CUCUMBER SLICES
1 CUP CARROT STICKS
1 CUP CHERRY TOMATOES
½ CUP BELL PEPPER STRIPS
(ANY COLOR)
¼ CUP HUMMUS (OPTIONAL,
FOR DIPPING)
PINCH OF SEA SALT AND BLACK
PEPPER (FOR EGGS)

INSTRUCTIONS:

Place eggs in a saucepan and cover with cold water. Bring to a boil, then reduce heat to low and simmer for 10–12 minutes. Drain and transfer eggs to an ice bath for 5 minutes. Peel once cooled.
Slice eggs in half and sprinkle lightly with salt and pepper.
Assemble snack boxes: divide eggs, cucumber, carrots, tomatoes, and bell peppers evenly into two meal-prep containers.
Add a small portion of hummus if desired. Keep refrigerated until ready to enjoy.
Clean Eating Tip
Prep several boxes at once for grab-and-go snacks during the week. Pair with whole grain crackers or fruit for a balanced mini meal.

 PREP TIME: **10 MIN**   COOK TIME: **12 MIN**   SERVINGS: **2**

Spinach & Mushroom Scramble

INGREDIENTS:

4 LARGE EGGS (OR 3 EGGS + 3 EGG WHITES
FOR LIGHTER OPTION)
2 TABLESPOONS UNSWEETENED ALMOND
MILK (OR WATER)
1 TABLESPOON OLIVE OIL OR AVOCADO OIL
1 CUP BABY SPINACH, ROUGHLY CHOPPED
1 CUP MUSHROOMS, SLICED (CREMINI,
BUTTON, OR YOUR FAVORITE)
2 TABLESPOONS CHOPPED ONION
(OPTIONAL)
¼ TEASPOON SEA SALT
⅛ TEASPOON BLACK PEPPER
OPTIONAL TOPPINGS: FRESH HERBS
(PARSLEY, CHIVES), SLICED AVOCADO, OR A
SPRINKLE OF FETA

INSTRUCTIONS:

In a bowl, whisk together eggs, almond milk, salt, and
pepper until fluffy.
Heat oil in a nonstick skillet over medium heat. Add
mushrooms (and onion if using) and sauté for 3–4 minutes
until softened.
Add spinach and cook for 1 minute, until wilted.
Pour the egg mixture over the vegetables. Gently stir with a
spatula, scraping the pan as the eggs cook, until soft and
just set (about 2–3 minutes).
Remove from heat and serve warm with desired toppings.
Clean Eating Tip
Cook eggs on low to medium heat for a softer texture and
avoid overcooking, which can make them rubbery.

 PREP TIME: **5 MIN**   COOK TIME: **10 MIN**   SERVINGS: **2**

Light & Refreshing
Salads

Chicken Quinoa Bowl *Recipe*

INGREDIENTS:

2 CANS (15 OZ EACH) CHICKPEAS, RINSED
AND DRAINED (OR 3 CUPS COOKED
CHICKPEAS)
1 ½ CUPS CUCUMBER, DICED
1 CUP CHERRY TOMATOES, HALVED
½ CUP RED BELL PEPPER, DICED
⅓ CUP RED ONION, FINELY CHOPPED
¼ CUP KALAMATA OLIVES, PITTED AND
SLICED
¼ CUP FETA CHEESE, CRUMBLED (OPTIONAL
FOR CLEAN VEGETARIAN VERSION)
3 TABLESPOONS EXTRA VIRGIN OLIVE OIL
2 TABLESPOONS FRESH LEMON JUICE
1 TABLESPOON RED WINE VINEGAR
1 TEASPOON DRIED OREGANO (OR 1
TABLESPOON FRESH, CHOPPED)
½ TEASPOON SEA SALT
¼ TEASPOON BLACK PEPPER
2 TABLESPOONS FRESH PARSLEY, CHOPPED

INSTRUCTIONS:

In a large bowl, combine chickpeas, cucumber, tomatoes, bell
pepper, onion, olives, and feta (if using).
In a small bowl or jar, whisk together olive oil, lemon juice,
vinegar, oregano, salt, and pepper.
Pour the dressing over the salad and toss until well coated.
Garnish with fresh parsley. Serve immediately or refrigerate for up
to 3 days.
Clean Eating Tip
Use dried chickpeas cooked from scratch for the cleanest option
— they're lower in sodium and have better texture than canned.

 PREP TIME: **20 MIN**

 SERVINGS: **4**

Quinoa & Roasted Vegetable Salad

INGREDIENTS:

1 CUP UNCOOKED QUINOA, RINSED
2 CUPS WATER OR LOW-SODIUM
VEGETABLE BROTH
1 MEDIUM ZUCCHINI, DICED
1 RED BELL PEPPER, DICED
1 YELLOW BELL PEPPER, DICED
1 SMALL RED ONION, CUT INTO
WEDGES
1 CUP CHERRY TOMATOES, HALVED
2 TABLESPOONS OLIVE OIL
1 TEASPOON DRIED OREGANO
½ TEASPOON SEA SALT
¼ TEASPOON BLACK PEPPER
2 TABLESPOONS FRESH LEMON
JUICE
2 TABLESPOONS FRESH PARSLEY
OR BASIL, CHOPPED

INSTRUCTIONS:

Preheat oven to 400°F (200°C). Line a baking sheet with parchment paper.

Toss zucchini, peppers, onion, and cherry tomatoes with olive oil, oregano, salt, and pepper. Spread evenly on the baking sheet. Roast for 20–25 minutes, stirring once, until tender and lightly caramelized.

While vegetables roast, combine quinoa and water (or broth) in a saucepan. Bring to a boil, then reduce heat to low, cover, and simmer for 15 minutes, until liquid is absorbed. Remove from heat and fluff with a fork.

In a large bowl, combine cooked quinoa, roasted vegetables, lemon juice, and fresh herbs. Toss gently to mix.

Serve warm, at room temperature, or chilled.

Clean Eating Tip

Make a double batch of quinoa and roasted veggies — they store well and can be used for wraps, bowls, or quick sides throughout the week.

 PREP TIME: **10 MIN**   COOK TIME: **25 MIN**   SERVINGS: **4**

Spinach, Strawberry & Walnut Salad

INGREDIENTS:

6 CUPS BABY SPINACH (ABOUT 5 OZ)
2 CUPS FRESH STRAWBERRIES,
HULLED AND SLICED
½ CUP WALNUTS, LIGHTLY TOASTED
¼ CUP RED ONION, THINLY SLICED
¼ CUP CRUMBLED FETA CHEESE
(OPTIONAL)
FOR THE DRESSING:
3 TABLESPOONS EXTRA VIRGIN OLIVE
OIL
2 TABLESPOONS BALSAMIC VINEGAR
1 TEASPOON DIJON MUSTARD
1 TEASPOON PURE MAPLE SYRUP OR
HONEY (OPTIONAL, TO BALANCE
ACIDITY)
PINCH OF SEA SALT
PINCH OF BLACK PEPPER

INSTRUCTIONS:

In a large salad bowl, combine spinach, strawberries, walnuts,
red onion, and feta (if using).
In a small jar or bowl, whisk together olive oil, balsamic vinegar,
Dijon mustard, maple syrup, salt, and pepper until emulsified.
Drizzle dressing over salad just before serving and toss gently to
coat.
Clean Eating Tip
Toast walnuts in a dry skillet over medium heat for 3–4 minutes
to enhance their flavor and crunch. Swap strawberries for
blueberries, raspberries, or pear slices depending on the
season.

 PREP TIME: **10 MIN**   SERVINGS: **2**

Cucumber & Tomato Refresh Salad

INGREDIENTS:

2 CUPS CUCUMBER, SLICED OR
DICED
2 CUPS CHERRY TOMATOES,
HALVED
¼ CUP RED ONION, THINLY SLICED
2 TABLESPOONS FRESH PARSLEY,
CHOPPED
2 TABLESPOONS EXTRA VIRGIN
OLIVE OIL
1 TABLESPOON FRESH LEMON
JUICE
½ TEASPOON SEA SALT
¼ TEASPOON BLACK PEPPER

INSTRUCTIONS:

In a large bowl, combine cucumber, cherry tomatoes, red
onion, and parsley.
In a small bowl or jar, whisk together olive oil, lemon juice,
salt, and pepper.
Pour the dressing over the vegetables and toss gently to
coat.
Serve immediately or chill for 10–15 minutes for a cooler,
more refreshing taste.
Clean Eating Tip
Use fresh, ripe cucumbers and tomatoes for the best flavor.
Add a few fresh herbs like basil or dill for extra freshness and
nutrients.

 PREP TIME: **10 MIN**

 SERVINGS:4

Chicken Quinoa Bowl *Recipe*

INGREDIENTS:

4 CUPS KALE, FINELY CHOPPED
(STEMS REMOVED)
1 MEDIUM APPLE, THINLY SLICED
OR JULIENNED
½ CUP SHREDDED CARROTS
¼ CUP RED CABBAGE, THINLY
SLICED (OPTIONAL FOR COLOR)
2 TABLESPOONS FRESH LEMON
JUICE
1 TABLESPOON EXTRA VIRGIN
OLIVE OIL
1 TEASPOON HONEY OR MAPLE
SYRUP (OPTIONAL)
¼ TEASPOON SEA SALT
⅛ TEASPOON BLACK PEPPER

INSTRUCTIONS:

In a large bowl, combine kale, apple, carrots, and red
cabbage (if using).
In a small bowl, whisk together lemon juice, olive oil, honey (if
using), salt, and pepper.
Pour dressing over the slaw and toss thoroughly to coat.
Let sit for 5–10 minutes before serving to allow flavors to
meld.
Clean Eating Tip
Massage the kale lightly with a pinch of salt before adding
dressing to soften the leaves and make them more tender.
This also improves digestibility.

 PREP TIME: **10 MIN**

 SERVINGS: **4**

Greek Salad with Olive Oil & Herbs

INGREDIENTS:

3 CUPS CUCUMBER, DICED
2 CUPS CHERRY TOMATOES, HALVED
1 RED BELL PEPPER, DICED
½ RED ONION, THINLY SLICED
¼ CUP KALAMATA OLIVES, PITTED AND HALVED
¼ CUP FETA CHEESE, CRUMBLED (OPTIONAL)
3 TABLESPOONS EXTRA VIRGIN OLIVE OIL
1 TABLESPOON RED WINE VINEGAR
1 TEASPOON DRIED OREGANO (OR 1 TABLESPOON FRESH, CHOPPED)
½ TEASPOON SEA SALT
¼ TEASPOON BLACK PEPPER
2 TABLESPOONS FRESH PARSLEY, CHOPPED

INSTRUCTIONS:

In a large bowl, combine cucumber, cherry tomatoes, bell pepper, red onion, olives, and feta (if using).
In a small bowl or jar, whisk together olive oil, red wine vinegar, oregano, salt, and pepper.
Pour the dressing over the salad and toss gently to coat.
Garnish with fresh parsley and serve immediately.
Clean Eating Tip
Use extra virgin olive oil for the healthiest fats and flavor. Omit feta for a fully plant-based version while keeping the Mediterranean freshness.

 PREP TIME: **10 MIN**   SERVINGS: **4**

Avocado & Black Bean Salad

INGREDIENTS:

1 CAN (15 OZ) BLACK BEANS, RINSED
AND DRAINED (OR 1 ½ CUPS
COOKED BLACK BEANS)
1 MEDIUM AVOCADO, DICED
1 CUP CHERRY TOMATOES, HALVED
½ CUP RED BELL PEPPER, DICED
¼ CUP RED ONION, FINELY CHOPPED
2 TABLESPOONS FRESH CILANTRO,
CHOPPED
2 TABLESPOONS FRESH LIME JUICE
1 TABLESPOON EXTRA VIRGIN OLIVE
OIL
½ TEASPOON GROUND CUMIN
½ TEASPOON SEA SALT
¼ TEASPOON BLACK PEPPER

INSTRUCTIONS:

In a large bowl, combine black beans, avocado, cherry
tomatoes, bell pepper, red onion, and cilantro.
In a small bowl, whisk together lime juice, olive oil, cumin,
salt, and pepper.
Pour dressing over the salad and gently toss to combine.
Serve immediately or chill for 10–15 minutes for flavors to
meld.
Clean Eating Tip
For the freshest flavor, use ripe, firm avocado and freshly
squeezed lime juice. This salad works well as a side, light
lunch, or protein-packed topping for greens.

 PREP TIME: **10 MIN**

 SERVINGS: **4**

Chicken Quinoa Bowl *Recipe*

INGREDIENTS:

2 MEDIUM ZUCCHINI, THINLY SLICED
INTO RIBBONS (USING A VEGETABLE
PEELER OR SPIRALIZER)
1 TABLESPOON EXTRA VIRGIN OLIVE
OIL
1 TABLESPOON FRESH LEMON JUICE
1 TEASPOON LEMON ZEST
2 TABLESPOONS FRESH PARSLEY,
CHOPPED
2 TABLESPOONS TOASTED
ALMONDS OR PINE NUTS
(OPTIONAL)
PINCH OF SEA SALT
PINCH OF BLACK PEPPER

INSTRUCTIONS:

Arrange zucchini ribbons in a large bowl or on a serving plate.
In a small bowl, whisk together olive oil, lemon juice, lemon zest,
salt, and pepper.
Drizzle the dressing over the zucchini ribbons and gently toss to
coat.
Sprinkle with parsley and toasted nuts (if using) before serving.
Clean Eating Tip
Use fresh, firm zucchini and a microplane for zesting the lemon to
maximize flavor without added calories. Serve immediately for a
crisp texture or let sit 5 minutes for a slightly softer salad.

 PREP TIME: **10 MIN**

 2–3
SERVINGS

Roasted Beet & Arugula Salad

INGREDIENTS:

4 MEDIUM BEETS, PEELED AND CUT
INTO WEDGES
1 TABLESPOON OLIVE OIL
PINCH OF SEA SALT
PINCH OF BLACK PEPPER
4 CUPS ARUGULA
¼ CUP WALNUTS, TOASTED
¼ CUP CRUMBLED GOAT CHEESE OR
FETA (OPTIONAL)
2 TABLESPOONS BALSAMIC VINEGAR
1 TABLESPOON EXTRA VIRGIN OLIVE
OIL
1 TEASPOON DIJON MUSTARD

INSTRUCTIONS:

Preheat oven to 400°F (200°C). Toss beet wedges with olive oil, salt, and pepper. Spread on a baking sheet and roast for 30–35 minutes, turning once, until tender. Let cool slightly.
In a large bowl, combine arugula and roasted beets.
In a small bowl, whisk together balsamic vinegar, olive oil, and Dijon mustard.
Drizzle dressing over the salad and toss gently to combine.
Top with toasted walnuts and crumbled cheese, if using. Serve immediately.
Clean Eating Tip
Roast beets with the skins on and peel after cooking to retain more nutrients. Add extra herbs like thyme or parsley for enhanced flavor without added calories.

 PREP TIME: **10 MIN**   COOK TIME: **40 MIN**   SERVINGS: **4**

Wholesome Soups & Stews

23

Classic Vegetable Soup

INGREDIENTS:

1 TABLESPOON OLIVE OIL
1 MEDIUM ONION, DICED
2 GARLIC CLOVES, MINCED
2 CARROTS, DICED
2 CELERY STALKS, DICED
1 ZUCCHINI, DICED
1 RED BELL PEPPER, DICED
1 CUP GREEN BEANS, TRIMMED AND
CHOPPED
1 CAN (14.5 OZ) DICED TOMATOES
6 CUPS LOW-SODIUM VEGETABLE BROTH
1 TEASPOON DRIED THYME
1 TEASPOON DRIED OREGANO
½ TEASPOON SEA SALT (ADJUST TO TASTE)
¼ TEASPOON BLACK PEPPER
2 CUPS FRESH SPINACH OR KALE, CHOPPED
OPTIONAL: FRESH PARSLEY FOR GARNISH

INSTRUCTIONS:

Heat olive oil in a large pot over medium heat. Add onion, garlic, carrots, and celery; sauté for 5–6 minutes until softened.
Add zucchini, bell pepper, and green beans; cook for 3–4 minutes.
Stir in diced tomatoes, vegetable broth, thyme, oregano, salt, and pepper. Bring to a boil, then reduce heat and simmer for 25 minutes, until vegetables are tender.
Stir in spinach or kale and cook for another 2–3 minutes.
Adjust seasoning as needed. Garnish with fresh parsley before serving.
Clean Eating Tip
Use a variety of colorful vegetables for maximum nutrients and fiber. This soup freezes well for up to 3 months, making it perfect for meal prep.

 PREP TIME: **10 MIN**   COOK TIME: **35 MIN**   SERVINGS: **6**

Hearty Lentil Stew

INGREDIENTS:

1 TABLESPOON OLIVE OIL
1 MEDIUM ONION, DICED
2 CARROTS, DICED
2 CELERY STALKS, DICED
3 GARLIC CLOVES, MINCED
1 TEASPOON GROUND CUMIN
1 TEASPOON SMOKED PAPRIKA
1 CUP BROWN OR GREEN LENTILS,
RINSED
1 CAN (14.5 OZ) DICED TOMATOES
4 CUPS LOW-SODIUM VEGETABLE
BROTH
1 BAY LEAF
1 TEASPOON DRIED THYME
2 CUPS CHOPPED KALE OR
SPINACH
SALT AND BLACK PEPPER, TO TASTE
OPTIONAL: FRESH PARSLEY FOR
GARNISH

INSTRUCTIONS:

Heat olive oil in a large pot over medium heat. Add onion, carrots, and celery; sauté for 5–6 minutes until softened.
Stir in garlic, cumin, and smoked paprika; cook for 1 minute until fragrant.
Add lentils, diced tomatoes, vegetable broth, bay leaf, and thyme. Bring to a boil, then reduce heat and simmer for 30–35 minutes, until lentils are tender.
Remove bay leaf, stir in kale or spinach, and cook 2–3 minutes until wilted.
Season with salt and pepper. Garnish with fresh parsley before serving.
Clean Eating Tip
For added depth of flavor, roast the vegetables in the oven before adding them to the stew. This stew keeps well in the fridge for 4–5 days and freezes beautifully for future meals.

 PREP TIME: **10 MIN**   COOK TIME: **40 MIN**   SERVINGS: **6**

Butternut Squash Soup

INGREDIENTS:

1 MEDIUM BUTTERNUT SQUASH (ABOUT
2–3 LBS), PEELED, SEEDED, AND CUBED
1 TABLESPOON OLIVE OIL
1 MEDIUM ONION, DICED
2 GARLIC CLOVES, MINCED
4 CUPS LOW-SODIUM VEGETABLE BROTH
1 TEASPOON GROUND CINNAMON
½ TEASPOON GROUND NUTMEG
½ TEASPOON SEA SALT (ADJUST TO
TASTE)
¼ TEASPOON BLACK PEPPER
½ CUP UNSWEETENED ALMOND MILK
(OR OTHER PLANT-BASED MILK,
OPTIONAL FOR CREAMINESS)
OPTIONAL TOPPINGS: PUMPKIN SEEDS,
FRESH PARSLEY, OR A DRIZZLE OF OLIVE
OIL

INSTRUCTIONS:

Heat olive oil in a large pot over medium heat. Sauté onion and garlic for
3–4 minutes until softened.
Add butternut squash, vegetable broth, cinnamon, nutmeg, salt, and
pepper. Bring to a boil, then reduce heat and simmer for 20–25 minutes,
until squash is tender.
Remove from heat and use an immersion blender to puree the soup
until smooth (or transfer in batches to a blender).
Stir in almond milk for added creaminess, if desired. Adjust seasoning as
needed.
Serve warm, topped with pumpkin seeds, parsley, or a drizzle of olive oil.
Clean Eating Tip
Roast the butternut squash for 20 minutes before adding to the pot to
enhance the natural sweetness and depth of flavor without added
sugars.

 PREP TIME: **10 MIN**   COOK TIME: **40 MIN**   SERVINGS: **4**

Chicken & Vegetable Soup

INGREDIENTS:

1 TABLESPOON OLIVE OIL
1 MEDIUM ONION, DICED
2 CARROTS, DICED
2 CELERY STALKS, DICED
2 GARLIC CLOVES, MINCED
1 LB BONELESS, SKINLESS CHICKEN
BREAST, CUT INTO BITE-SIZED PIECES
6 CUPS LOW-SODIUM CHICKEN OR
VEGETABLE BROTH
1 CUP GREEN BEANS, TRIMMED AND
CHOPPED
1 ZUCCHINI, DICED
1 TEASPOON DRIED THYME
½ TEASPOON DRIED ROSEMARY
½ TEASPOON SEA SALT (ADJUST TO TASTE)
¼ TEASPOON BLACK PEPPER
2 CUPS FRESH SPINACH OR KALE,
CHOPPED
OPTIONAL: FRESH PARSLEY FOR GARNISH

INSTRUCTIONS:

Heat olive oil in a large pot over medium heat. Add onion, carrots, and celery; sauté for 5–6 minutes until softened.
Add garlic and cook for 1 minute until fragrant.
Stir in chicken pieces and cook for 3–4 minutes until lightly browned on the outside.
Add broth, green beans, zucchini, thyme, rosemary, salt, and pepper. Bring to a boil, then reduce heat and simmer for 20 minutes, until chicken is cooked through and vegetables are tender.
Stir in spinach or kale and cook 2–3 minutes until wilted.
Adjust seasoning as needed and garnish with fresh parsley before serving.
Clean Eating Tip
Use fresh, high-quality chicken and a variety of colorful vegetables for maximum nutrients. This soup keeps well in the fridge for up to 4 days and freezes beautifully for future meals.

 PREP TIME: **10 MIN**   COOK TIME: **35 MIN**   SERVINGS: **6**

Tomato Basil Soup

INGREDIENTS:

1 TABLESPOON OLIVE OIL
1 MEDIUM ONION, DICED
2 GARLIC CLOVES, MINCED
1 CAN (28 OZ) WHOLE PEELED
TOMATOES, UNDRAINED
1 CUP LOW-SODIUM VEGETABLE
BROTH
1 TEASPOON DRIED OREGANO
½ TEASPOON SEA SALT (ADJUST TO
TASTE)
¼ TEASPOON BLACK PEPPER
½ CUP FRESH BASIL LEAVES,
CHOPPED
OPTIONAL: ¼ CUP UNSWEETENED
ALMOND MILK OR COCONUT MILK
FOR CREAMINESS

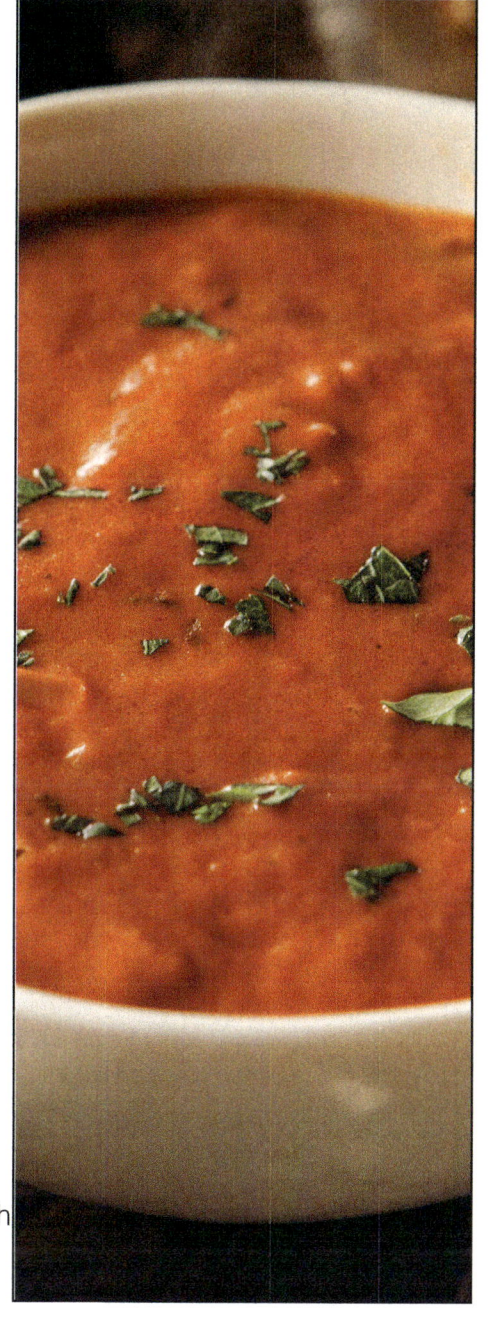

INSTRUCTIONS:

Heat olive oil in a large pot over medium heat. Sauté onion for 4–5 minutes until softened, then add garlic and cook 1 minute until fragrant.

Add tomatoes (with juice), vegetable broth, oregano, salt, and pepper. Bring to a boil, then reduce heat and simmer for 15–20 minutes.

Remove from heat and use an immersion blender to puree until smooth (or transfer in batches to a blender).

Stir in fresh basil and optional almond or coconut milk for creaminess. Adjust seasoning as needed.

Serve warm, garnished with extra basil leaves if desired.

Clean Eating Tip

Use fresh basil for vibrant flavor and maximum antioxidants. Pair with whole-grain toast or a side salad for a complete, healthy meal.

 PREP TIME: **10 MIN**   COOK TIME: **25 MIN**   SERVINGS: **4**

Sweet Potato & Carrot Soup

INGREDIENTS:

1 TABLESPOON OLIVE OIL
1 MEDIUM ONION, DICED
2 GARLIC CLOVES, MINCED
2 MEDIUM SWEET POTATOES, PEELED AND DICED
3 MEDIUM CARROTS, PEELED AND DICED
4 CUPS LOW-SODIUM VEGETABLE BROTH
1 TEASPOON GROUND GINGER
½ TEASPOON GROUND CINNAMON
½ TEASPOON SEA SALT (ADJUST TO TASTE)
¼ TEASPOON BLACK PEPPER
OPTIONAL: ¼ CUP UNSWEETENED COCONUT MILK FOR CREAMINESS
OPTIONAL GARNISH: FRESH PARSLEY OR A DRIZZLE OF OLIVE OIL

INSTRUCTIONS:

Heat olive oil in a large pot over medium heat. Sauté onion for 4–5 minutes until softened, then add garlic and cook 1 minute until fragrant.

Add sweet potatoes, carrots, vegetable broth, ginger, cinnamon, salt, and pepper. Bring to a boil, then reduce heat and simmer for 20–25 minutes until vegetables are tender.

Remove from heat and use an immersion blender to puree the soup until smooth (or transfer in batches to a blender).

Stir in coconut milk if using, and adjust seasoning to taste.

Serve warm, garnished with parsley or a drizzle of olive oil if desired.

Clean Eating Tip

Roast the sweet potatoes and carrots before adding them to the pot to enhance natural sweetness without added sugar. This soup also freezes well for easy meal prep.

 PREP TIME: **10 MIN**   COOK TIME: **30 MIN**   SERVINGS: **4**

Quinoa & Kale Soup

INGREDIENTS:

1 TABLESPOON OLIVE OIL
1 MEDIUM ONION, DICED
2 GARLIC CLOVES, MINCED
2 CARROTS, DICED
2 CELERY STALKS, DICED
1 TEASPOON DRIED THYME
1 TEASPOON DRIED OREGANO
1 CUP QUINOA, RINSED
6 CUPS LOW-SODIUM VEGETABLE BROTH
2 CUPS CHOPPED KALE, STEMS
REMOVED
1 CAN (14.5 OZ) DICED TOMATOES
½ TEASPOON SEA SALT (ADJUST TO
TASTE)
¼ TEASPOON BLACK PEPPER
OPTIONAL: FRESH PARSLEY OR LEMON
JUICE FOR GARNISH

INSTRUCTIONS:

Heat olive oil in a large pot over medium heat. Add onion, garlic, carrots, and celery; sauté for 5–6 minutes until softened.
Stir in thyme and oregano; cook 1 minute until fragrant.
Add quinoa, vegetable broth, and diced tomatoes. Bring to a boil, then reduce heat and simmer for 15 minutes.
Stir in chopped kale and cook for another 5 minutes until wilted.
Season with salt and pepper, and garnish with fresh parsley or a squeeze of lemon juice before serving.
Clean Eating Tip
Rinse quinoa thoroughly before cooking to remove natural bitterness. This soup is rich in protein, fiber, and antioxidants, making it a hearty, nutrient-dense meal.

 PREP TIME: **10 MIN**   COOK TIME: **25 MIN**   SERVINGS: 4

Mushroom Barley Stew

INGREDIENTS:

1 TABLESPOON OLIVE OIL
1 MEDIUM ONION, DICED
2 GARLIC CLOVES, MINCED
2 CARROTS, DICED
2 CELERY STALKS, DICED
10 OZ MUSHROOMS, SLICED (BUTTON,
CREMINI, OR A MIX)
1 CUP PEARL BARLEY, RINSED
6 CUPS LOW-SODIUM VEGETABLE BROTH
1 TEASPOON DRIED THYME
1 TEASPOON DRIED ROSEMARY
½ TEASPOON SEA SALT (ADJUST TO
TASTE)
¼ TEASPOON BLACK PEPPER
2 CUPS CHOPPED KALE OR SPINACH
OPTIONAL: FRESH PARSLEY FOR GARNISH

INSTRUCTIONS:

Heat olive oil in a large pot over medium heat. Add onion, garlic, carrots, and celery; sauté for 5–6 minutes until softened.
Add mushrooms and cook for another 5 minutes until they release their moisture.
Stir in barley, vegetable broth, thyme, rosemary, salt, and pepper.
Bring to a boil, then reduce heat and simmer, covered, for 35–40 minutes, until barley is tender.
Stir in kale or spinach and cook for 2–3 minutes until wilted.
Adjust seasoning as needed and garnish with fresh parsley before serving.
Clean Eating Tip
Rinse barley thoroughly before cooking to remove excess starch.
This stew is high in fiber, plant-based protein, and packed with earthy flavors, making it perfect for a filling, nutritious meal.

 PREP TIME: **10 MIN**   COOK TIME: **35 MIN**   SERVINGS: **4-6**

Broccoli & Spinach Detox Soup

INGREDIENTS:

1 TABLESPOON OLIVE OIL
1 MEDIUM ONION, DICED
2 GARLIC CLOVES, MINCED
4 CUPS BROCCOLI FLORETS
2 CUPS FRESH SPINACH
4 CUPS LOW-SODIUM VEGETABLE
BROTH
1 TEASPOON GROUND TURMERIC
(OPTIONAL, FOR ADDED ANTI-
INFLAMMATORY BENEFITS)
½ TEASPOON SEA SALT (ADJUST TO
TASTE)
¼ TEASPOON BLACK PEPPER
OPTIONAL GARNISH: LEMON JUICE,
PUMPKIN SEEDS, OR FRESH PARSLEY

INSTRUCTIONS:

Heat olive oil in a large pot over medium heat. Sauté onion for 4–5 minutes until softened, then add garlic and cook 1 minute until fragrant.
Add broccoli, vegetable broth, turmeric, salt, and pepper. Bring to a boil, then reduce heat and simmer for 10–12 minutes until broccoli is tender.
Stir in fresh spinach and cook for 2–3 minutes until wilted.
Use an immersion blender to puree the soup until smooth, or transfer in batches to a blender.
Adjust seasoning as needed and serve warm, garnished with lemon juice, pumpkin seeds, or parsley if desired.
Clean Eating Tip
This detox soup is naturally low in calories but high in vitamins, minerals, and antioxidants. Pair it with a slice of whole-grain toast or a side salad for a balanced, nourishing meal.

 PREP TIME: **10 MIN**   COOK TIME: **20 MIN**   SERVINGS: **4**

White Bean & Rosemary Soup

INGREDIENTS:

1 TABLESPOON OLIVE OIL
1 MEDIUM ONION, DICED
2 GARLIC CLOVES, MINCED
2 CARROTS, DICED
2 CELERY STALKS, DICED
1 CAN (15 OZ) WHITE BEANS, RINSED
AND DRAINED (OR 1 ½ CUPS COOKED
BEANS)
4 CUPS LOW-SODIUM VEGETABLE
BROTH
1 TEASPOON FRESH OR DRIED
ROSEMARY
½ TEASPOON SEA SALT (ADJUST TO
TASTE)
¼ TEASPOON BLACK PEPPER
2 CUPS CHOPPED KALE OR SPINACH
OPTIONAL GARNISH: FRESH PARSLEY
OR A DRIZZLE OF OLIVE OIL

INSTRUCTIONS:

Heat olive oil in a large pot over medium heat. Add onion, garlic, carrots, and celery; sauté for 5–6 minutes until softened.
Stir in white beans, vegetable broth, rosemary, salt, and pepper. Bring to a boil, then reduce heat and simmer for 20 minutes to allow flavors to meld.
Add chopped kale or spinach and cook for another 2–3 minutes until wilted.
Adjust seasoning as needed and serve warm, garnished with parsley or a drizzle of olive oil if desired.
Clean Eating Tip
Use dried beans cooked from scratch for the cleanest option, or rinse canned beans thoroughly to reduce sodium. This soup is high in fiber and plant-based protein, making it a filling and wholesome meal.

 PREP TIME: **10 MIN**   COOK TIME: **30 MIN**   SERVINGS: **4-6**

Simple & Nourishing Lunches

34

Grilled Chicken & Veggie Wrap

INGREDIENTS:

2 WHOLE GRAIN OR SPROUTED
GRAIN TORTILLAS
1 CUP COOKED GRILLED
CHICKEN BREAST, SLICED
½ CUP BELL PEPPERS, THINLY
SLICED
½ CUP CUCUMBER, THINLY
SLICED
½ CUP SHREDDED CARROTS
¼ CUP HUMMUS OR MASHED
AVOCADO
1 CUP BABY SPINACH OR MIXED
GREENS
OPTIONAL: A SQUEEZE OF
LEMON JUICE OR SPRINKLE OF
BLACK PEPPER

INSTRUCTIONS:

Warm tortillas in a skillet or microwave for 20–30 seconds to
make them pliable.
Spread hummus or mashed avocado evenly over each tortilla.
Layer sliced chicken, bell peppers, cucumber, carrots, and
greens on top.
Roll the tortilla tightly to form a wrap and slice in half if desired.
Serve immediately, or wrap in parchment paper for a portable
meal.
Clean Eating Tip
Use sprouted grain tortillas for extra fiber and protein. Grill
chicken with minimal oil and season with herbs rather than
high-sodium sauces for a healthier option.

 PREP TIME: **10 MIN**   COOK TIME: **10 MIN**   SERVINGS: **2**

Brown Rice Buddha Bowl

INGREDIENTS:

1 CUP COOKED BROWN RICE
1 CUP ROASTED OR STEAMED
BROCCOLI FLORETS
1 CUP ROASTED SWEET POTATO CUBES
½ CUP SHREDDED CARROTS
½ CUP CHICKPEAS, ROASTED OR
LIGHTLY SAUTÉED
¼ AVOCADO, SLICED PER BOWL
2 TABLESPOONS TAHINI OR HUMMUS
1 TABLESPOON LEMON JUICE
1 TEASPOON OLIVE OIL
SALT AND BLACK PEPPER, TO TASTE
OPTIONAL TOPPINGS: SESAME SEEDS,
PUMPKIN SEEDS, OR FRESH HERBS

INSTRUCTIONS:

Prepare all vegetables by roasting or steaming until tender.
Divide cooked brown rice between two bowls.
Arrange broccoli, sweet potatoes, carrots, chickpeas, and
avocado on top of the rice.
Drizzle each bowl with tahini or hummus, lemon juice, and olive
oil. Season with salt and pepper.
Sprinkle optional seeds or fresh herbs for extra flavor and crunch.
Clean Eating Tip
Mix and match seasonal vegetables for variety. Using roasted
chickpeas adds plant-based protein and crunch without extra oil.
This bowl is perfect for meal prep, as components can be made
in advance and assembled quickly.

 PREP TIME: **10 MIN**   COOK TIME: **20 MIN**   SERVINGS: **2**

Baked Falafel with Tahini Dressing

INGREDIENTS:

1 CAN (15 OZ) CHICKPEAS, RINSED
AND DRAINED (OR 1 ½ CUPS COOKED
CHICKPEAS)
1 SMALL ONION, ROUGHLY CHOPPED
2 GARLIC CLOVES
¼ CUP FRESH PARSLEY
¼ CUP FRESH CILANTRO
2 TABLESPOONS WHOLE WHEAT
FLOUR OR CHICKPEA FLOUR
1 TEASPOON GROUND CUMIN
1 TEASPOON GROUND CORIANDER
½ TEASPOON BAKING POWDER
¼ TEASPOON SEA SALT
¼ TEASPOON BLACK PEPPER
FOR THE TAHINI DRESSING:
3 TABLESPOONS TAHINI
1 TABLESPOON FRESH LEMON JUICE
2–3 TABLESPOONS WATER (TO THIN
AS NEEDED)
PINCH OF SEA SALT

INSTRUCTIONS:

Preheat oven to 400°F (200°C) and line a baking sheet with parchment paper.
In a food processor, combine chickpeas, onion, garlic, parsley, cilantro, flour, cumin, coriander, baking powder, salt, and pepper. Pulse until a coarse mixture forms (do not over-process).
Form mixture into small patties or balls, about 1 ½ inches in diameter, and place on the prepared baking sheet.
Bake for 20–25 minutes, flipping halfway through, until golden and firm.
Meanwhile, whisk together tahini, lemon juice, water, and salt until smooth, adjusting water to desired consistency.
Serve baked falafel warm with tahini dressing, and optionally alongside a fresh salad or whole grain wrap.
Clean Eating Tip
Baking falafel instead of frying reduces added oils while keeping them flavorful. Use fresh herbs for vibrant taste and added nutrients.

 PREP TIME: **10 MIN**   COOK TIME: **25 MIN**   4 SERVINGS (MAKES ABOUT 12 FALAFEL PATTIES)

Salmon & Quinoa Bowl

INGREDIENTS:

1 CUP COOKED QUINOA
2 SALMON FILLETS (ABOUT 4–6
OZ EACH)
1 TABLESPOON OLIVE OIL
1 TEASPOON LEMON ZEST
1 TEASPOON PAPRIKA
½ TEASPOON SEA SALT
¼ TEASPOON BLACK PEPPER
1 CUP STEAMED BROCCOLI
FLORETS
½ CUP SHREDDED CARROTS
½ AVOCADO, SLICED
OPTIONAL: FRESH HERBS
(PARSLEY, CILANTRO, OR DILL)

INSTRUCTIONS:

Preheat oven to 400°F (200°C). Rub salmon fillets with olive oil,
lemon zest, paprika, salt, and pepper. Bake for 12–15 minutes until
cooked through.
Divide cooked quinoa between two bowls.
Arrange salmon, broccoli, carrots, and avocado on top of the quinoa.
Garnish with fresh herbs if desired and serve immediately.
Clean Eating Tip
Choose wild-caught salmon for higher omega-3 content. Mix up
vegetables based on seasonal availability for variety and optimal
nutrition.

 PREP TIME: **10 MIN**   COOK TIME: **25 MIN**   SERVINGS: **2**

Veggie Stir-Fry with Ginger Soy Sauce

INGREDIENTS:

1 TABLESPOON SESAME OIL OR OLIVE OIL
1 CUP BROCCOLI FLORETS
1 CUP BELL PEPPERS, SLICED
1 CUP SNAP PEAS OR GREEN BEANS
1 MEDIUM CARROT, THINLY SLICED
2 GARLIC CLOVES, MINCED
1 TEASPOON FRESH GINGER, GRATED
2 TABLESPOONS LOW-SODIUM SOY SAUCE OR TAMARI
1 TABLESPOON RICE VINEGAR
1 TEASPOON HONEY OR MAPLE SYRUP (OPTIONAL)
1 GREEN ONION, SLICED (FOR GARNISH)
OPTIONAL: SESAME SEEDS FOR GARNISH

INSTRUCTIONS:

Heat oil in a large skillet or wok over medium-high heat. Add broccoli, bell peppers, snap peas, and carrot. Stir-fry for 4–5 minutes until vegetables are crisp-tender.
Add garlic and ginger; cook for 1 minute until fragrant.
Stir in soy sauce, rice vinegar, and honey/maple syrup. Cook for another 1–2 minutes until vegetables are coated in sauce.
Serve immediately, garnished with green onion and sesame seeds.
Clean Eating Tip
Use a variety of colorful vegetables for maximum nutrients. Serve over brown rice, quinoa, or whole-grain noodles for a complete, balanced meal.

 PREP TIME: **10 MIN**   COOK TIME: **10 MIN**   SERVINGS: **2**

Lentil & Sweet Potato Tacos

INGREDIENTS:

1 TABLESPOON OLIVE OIL
1 MEDIUM ONION, DICED
2 GARLIC CLOVES, MINCED
1 TEASPOON GROUND CUMIN
1 TEASPOON SMOKED PAPRIKA
1 CAN (15 OZ) COOKED LENTILS,
RINSED AND DRAINED (OR 1 ½ CUPS
COOKED LENTILS)
1 MEDIUM SWEET POTATO, PEELED
AND DICED
¼ TEASPOON SEA SALT
¼ TEASPOON BLACK PEPPER
8 SMALL CORN OR WHOLE-GRAIN
TORTILLAS
OPTIONAL TOPPINGS: AVOCADO
SLICES, FRESH CILANTRO, SALSA, LIME
WEDGES, SHREDDED LETTUCE

INSTRUCTIONS:

Heat olive oil in a skillet over medium heat. Sauté onion and garlic for 3–4 minutes until softened.
Add cumin and smoked paprika; cook for 1 minute until fragrant.
Stir in lentils, sweet potato, salt, and pepper. Cook for 15–20 minutes, stirring occasionally, until sweet potatoes are tender.
Warm tortillas in a skillet or microwave.
Divide lentil and sweet potato mixture among tortillas and top with desired garnishes.
Serve immediately with lime wedges on the side.
Clean Eating Tip
Use corn or sprouted grain tortillas for extra fiber and nutrients. These tacos are naturally plant-based, high in protein, and packed with fiber from lentils and sweet potatoes.

 PREP TIME: **10 MIN**   COOK TIME: **25 MIN**   SERVINGS: **4**

Egg Salad with Avocado (no mayo)

INGREDIENTS:

4 LARGE HARD-BOILED EGGS,
PEELED AND CHOPPED
½ RIPE AVOCADO
1 TEASPOON DIJON MUSTARD
1 TEASPOON FRESH LEMON
JUICE
2 TABLESPOONS CHOPPED
FRESH CHIVES OR GREEN
ONION
SALT AND BLACK PEPPER, TO
TASTE
OPTIONAL: A PINCH OF
SMOKED PAPRIKA OR FRESH
HERBS FOR GARNISH

INSTRUCTIONS:

Mash avocado in a medium bowl until smooth.
Add chopped hard-boiled eggs, Dijon mustard, lemon
juice, and chives. Mix gently to combine.
Season with salt and pepper to taste.
Serve immediately on whole-grain toast, in a wrap, or as a
salad topping.
Garnish with smoked paprika or fresh herbs if desired.
Clean Eating Tip
Avocado replaces mayonnaise for healthy fats and
creaminess, keeping this classic dish light and nutrient-
dense. Prepare eggs ahead of time for quick meal prep.

 PREP TIME: **10 MIN**   COOK TIME: **10 MIN**   SERVINGS: **2**

Clean Eating Dinners

Lemon Herb Baked Salmon

INGREDIENTS:

2 SALMON FILLETS (4–6 OZ
EACH)
1 TABLESPOON OLIVE OIL
1 TEASPOON LEMON ZEST
1 TABLESPOON FRESH LEMON
JUICE
1 TEASPOON FRESH THYME
LEAVES (OR ½ TEASPOON
DRIED THYME)
1 TEASPOON FRESH PARSLEY,
CHOPPED
½ TEASPOON SEA SALT
¼ TEASPOON BLACK PEPPER

INSTRUCTIONS:

Preheat oven to 400°F (200°C). Line a baking sheet with
parchment paper.
Place salmon fillets on the prepared baking sheet.
Drizzle olive oil, lemon juice, and lemon zest over the
fillets. Sprinkle with thyme, parsley, salt, and pepper.
Bake for 12–15 minutes, or until salmon flakes easily with
a fork.
Serve immediately with your choice of vegetables,
grains, or a fresh salad.
Clean Eating Tip
Use wild-caught salmon for higher omega-3 content.
Pair with lightly steamed vegetables and whole grains for
a balanced, nutrient-dense meal.

 PREP TIME: **10 MIN**   COOK TIME: **20 MIN**   SERVINGS: **2**

Grilled Chicken with Roasted Veggies

INGREDIENTS:

2 BONELESS, SKINLESS
CHICKEN BREASTS (ABOUT 4–6
OZ EACH)
1 TABLESPOON OLIVE OIL,
DIVIDED
1 TEASPOON PAPRIKA
1 TEASPOON GARLIC POWDER
½ TEASPOON SEA SALT
¼ TEASPOON BLACK PEPPER
1 CUP BROCCOLI FLORETS
1 CUP BELL PEPPERS, SLICED
1 CUP ZUCCHINI, SLICED
1 TEASPOON FRESH THYME
OR ROSEMARY (OPTIONAL)

INSTRUCTIONS:

Preheat oven to 400°F (200°C). Toss broccoli, bell peppers, and zucchini with half the olive oil, salt, pepper, and herbs. Spread on a baking sheet and roast for 20–25 minutes until tender.
While vegetables roast, brush chicken breasts with remaining olive oil and season with paprika, garlic powder, salt, and pepper.
Grill chicken on a preheated grill or grill pan over medium heat for 6–7 minutes per side, until cooked through and juices run clear.
Serve grilled chicken alongside roasted vegetables.
Clean Eating Tip
Use a variety of colorful vegetables for maximum nutrients and fiber. Marinate chicken briefly in olive oil, lemon juice, and herbs for added flavor without extra sodium.

 PREP TIME: **10 MIN**   COOK TIME: **30 MIN**   SERVINGS: **2**

Turkey & Quinoa Stuffed Peppers

INGREDIENTS:

4 LARGE BELL PEPPERS, TOPS CUT
OFF AND SEEDS REMOVED
1 TABLESPOON OLIVE OIL
1 SMALL ONION, DICED
2 GARLIC CLOVES, MINCED
1 LB (450 G) LEAN GROUND TURKEY
1 CUP COOKED QUINOA
1 CAN (14.5 OZ) DICED TOMATOES,
DRAINED
1 TEASPOON DRIED OREGANO
1 TEASPOON PAPRIKA
½ TEASPOON SEA SALT
¼ TEASPOON BLACK PEPPER
¼ CUP FRESH PARSLEY, CHOPPED
OPTIONAL: ¼ CUP SHREDDED LOW-
FAT CHEESE

INSTRUCTIONS:

Preheat oven to 375°F (190°C).
Heat olive oil in a skillet over medium heat. Sauté onion and garlic for
3–4 minutes until softened.
Add ground turkey and cook until browned, breaking it into small
pieces. Stir in cooked quinoa, diced tomatoes, oregano, paprika, salt,
and pepper. Cook for 2–3 minutes until heated through.
Stuff each bell pepper with the turkey-quinoa mixture and place them
in a baking dish.
Cover with foil and bake for 25–30 minutes. Remove foil, sprinkle with
cheese if using, and bake for an additional 5 minutes until cheese is
melted and peppers are tender.
Garnish with fresh parsley before serving.
Clean Eating Tip
Use a variety of bell pepper colors for extra vitamins and antioxidants.
Lean turkey and quinoa provide a protein-rich filling while keeping this
meal nutrient-dense and low in saturated fat.

 PREP TIME: **10 MIN**   COOK TIME: **45 MIN**   4 SERVINGS
(4 PEPPERS)

Cauliflower Rice Stir-Fry

INGREDIENTS:

1 TABLESPOON SESAME OIL OR
OLIVE OIL
2 CUPS CAULIFLOWER RICE
(FRESH OR FROZEN)
1 CUP MIXED VEGETABLES (BELL
PEPPERS, CARROTS, PEAS, OR
BROCCOLI)
2 GARLIC CLOVES, MINCED
1 TEASPOON FRESH GINGER,
GRATED
2 TABLESPOONS LOW-SODIUM
SOY SAUCE OR TAMARI
1 TEASPOON RICE VINEGAR
2 GREEN ONIONS, SLICED
OPTIONAL: SESAME SEEDS OR
FRESH CILANTRO FOR GARNISH

INSTRUCTIONS:

Heat oil in a large skillet or wok over medium-high heat. Add
garlic and ginger; sauté for 1 minute until fragrant.
Add mixed vegetables and stir-fry for 3–4 minutes until crisp-
tender.
Stir in cauliflower rice, soy sauce, and rice vinegar. Cook for 3–4
minutes, stirring frequently, until heated through and slightly
tender.
Remove from heat and top with green onions, sesame seeds, or
fresh cilantro. Serve immediately.
Clean Eating Tip
Use a variety of colorful vegetables for maximum nutrients.
Cauliflower rice is a low-carb alternative to traditional rice and
adds extra fiber and vitamins. This dish works well as a quick
weeknight dinner or meal prep option.

 PREP TIME: **10 MIN**   COOK TIME: **10 MIN**   SERVINGS: **2**

Zucchini Noodles with Pesto

INGREDIENTS:

2 MEDIUM ZUCCHINIS, SPIRALIZED INTO NOODLES
2 TABLESPOONS OLIVE OIL
½ CUP FRESH BASIL LEAVES
2 TABLESPOONS PINE NUTS OR WALNUTS
1 GARLIC CLOVE
2 TABLESPOONS NUTRITIONAL YEAST (OR PARMESAN CHEESE, OPTIONAL)
2 TEASPOONS LEMON JUICE
SALT AND BLACK PEPPER, TO TASTE
OPTIONAL TOPPINGS: CHERRY TOMATOES, ROASTED CHICKPEAS, OR EXTRA NUTS

INSTRUCTIONS:

In a food processor or blender, combine basil, pine nuts, garlic, nutritional yeast, lemon juice, olive oil, salt, and pepper. Blend until smooth to make the pesto. Adjust consistency with a little water if needed.

Heat a skillet over medium heat. Add zucchini noodles and sauté for 2–3 minutes until just tender (avoid overcooking to prevent sogginess).

Toss zucchini noodles with pesto until evenly coated.

Serve immediately, topped with cherry tomatoes, roasted chickpeas, or extra nuts if desired.

Clean Eating Tip

Use fresh, firm zucchini for the best texture. Nutritional yeast adds a cheesy flavor while keeping this meal dairy-free and nutrient-dense.

 PREP TIME: **10 MIN**   COOK TIME: **10 MIN**   SERVINGS: **2**

Black Bean Veggie Burgers

INGREDIENTS:

1 CAN (15 OZ) BLACK BEANS, RINSED AND DRAINED (OR 1 ½ CUPS COOKED BLACK BEANS)
½ CUP ROLLED OATS OR OAT FLOUR
1 SMALL CARROT, GRATED
½ SMALL ONION, FINELY DICED
2 GARLIC CLOVES, MINCED
1 TEASPOON GROUND CUMIN
1 TEASPOON SMOKED PAPRIKA
½ TEASPOON SEA SALT
¼ TEASPOON BLACK PEPPER
1 TABLESPOON OLIVE OIL (FOR COOKING)
OPTIONAL TOPPINGS: AVOCADO, LETTUCE, TOMATO, WHOLE-GRAIN BUN, OR YOUR FAVORITE SAUCE

INSTRUCTIONS:

In a large bowl, mash black beans until mostly smooth, leaving some texture.
Stir in oats, carrot, onion, garlic, cumin, paprika, salt, and pepper until well combined. If mixture is too wet, add a little more oats; if too dry, add 1–2 teaspoons water.
Form mixture into 4 patties.
Heat olive oil in a skillet over medium heat. Cook patties for 4–5 minutes per side, until golden brown and heated through.
Serve on whole-grain buns or over a salad, and top with avocado, lettuce, or tomato as desired.
Clean Eating Tip
Using oats instead of breadcrumbs keeps these burgers whole-grain and fiber-rich. Customize with your favorite vegetables or spices for variety and extra nutrients.

 PREP TIME: **10 MIN**   COOK TIME: **10 MIN**   4 SERVINGS (4 PATTIES)

Slow-Baked Cod with Garlic & Herbs

INGREDIENTS:

2 COD FILLETS (4–6 OZ EACH)
2 TABLESPOONS OLIVE OIL
2 GARLIC CLOVES, MINCED
1 TEASPOON FRESH THYME
LEAVES (OR ½ TEASPOON
DRIED THYME)
1 TEASPOON FRESH PARSLEY,
CHOPPED
1 TEASPOON LEMON ZEST
2 TABLESPOONS FRESH LEMON
JUICE
½ TEASPOON SEA SALT
¼ TEASPOON BLACK PEPPER

INSTRUCTIONS:

Preheat oven to 300°F (150°C). Lightly grease a baking dish.
Place cod fillets in the dish and drizzle with olive oil and lemon
juice.
Sprinkle with garlic, thyme, parsley, lemon zest, salt, and pepper.
Cover loosely with foil and bake for 20–25 minutes, or until the fish
flakes easily with a fork.
Serve immediately with a side of steamed vegetables, quinoa, or
a fresh salad.
Clean Eating Tip
Slow-baking at a lower temperature keeps cod moist and tender.
Pair with seasonal vegetables for a light, balanced meal.

 PREP TIME: **10 MIN**   COOK TIME: **25 MIN**    SERVINGS: **2**

Sheet Pan Chicken Fajitas

INGREDIENTS:

1 LB (450 G) BONELESS, SKINLESS
CHICKEN BREASTS, SLICED INTO THIN
STRIPS
2 BELL PEPPERS, SLICED (ANY COLOR)
1 MEDIUM RED ONION, SLICED
2 TABLESPOONS OLIVE OIL
1 TEASPOON CHILI POWDER
1 TEASPOON SMOKED PAPRIKA
1 TEASPOON CUMIN
½ TEASPOON GARLIC POWDER
½ TEASPOON SEA SALT
¼ TEASPOON BLACK PEPPER
JUICE OF 1 LIME
OPTIONAL FOR SERVING: WHOLE-GRAIN
TORTILLAS, AVOCADO, SALSA, OR GREEK
YOGURT

INSTRUCTIONS:

Preheat oven to 400°F (200°C). Line a large baking sheet with
parchment paper.
Place chicken, bell peppers, and onion on the baking sheet.
Drizzle with olive oil and sprinkle with chili powder, paprika, cumin,
garlic powder, salt, and pepper. Toss to coat evenly.
Spread into a single layer and bake for 20–25 minutes, stirring
halfway, until chicken is cooked through and vegetables are
tender.
Squeeze lime juice over the mixture before serving.
Serve in whole-grain tortillas with avocado, salsa, or Greek
yogurt, if desired.
Clean Eating Tip
Using a sheet pan makes this meal quick and low-maintenance,
with minimal cleanup. Opt for whole-grain or corn tortillas to boost
fiber and keep the dish nutrient-dense.

 PREP TIME: **10 MIN**   COOK TIME: **20 MIN**   SERVINGS: **4**

Veggie-Packed Turkey Meatballs

INGREDIENTS:

1 LB (450 G) LEAN GROUND TURKEY
1 SMALL ZUCCHINI, GRATED AND EXCESS
MOISTURE SQUEEZED OUT
1 SMALL CARROT, GRATED
½ SMALL ONION, FINELY DICED
2 GARLIC CLOVES, MINCED
½ CUP ROLLED OATS (BLENDED INTO OAT
FLOUR) OR WHOLE-WHEAT
BREADCRUMBS
1 EGG, LIGHTLY BEATEN
1 TEASPOON DRIED OREGANO
½ TEASPOON PAPRIKA
½ TEASPOON SEA SALT
¼ TEASPOON BLACK PEPPER
1 TABLESPOON OLIVE OIL (FOR BAKING
SHEET OR PAN)

INSTRUCTIONS:

Preheat oven to 400°F (200°C). Lightly grease a baking sheet with olive oil or line with parchment paper.
In a large bowl, combine ground turkey, zucchini, carrot, onion, garlic, oats, egg, oregano, paprika, salt, and pepper. Mix gently until just combined.
Form mixture into 1-inch meatballs and place on the prepared baking sheet.
Bake for 18–20 minutes, or until cooked through and golden brown.
Serve with marinara sauce over whole-grain pasta, zucchini noodles, or as a protein-packed snack.
Clean Eating Tip
Adding vegetables to meatballs boosts nutrients and fiber while keeping them moist. Baking instead of frying reduces extra oil while still creating a flavorful, hearty meal.

 PREP TIME: **10 MIN**   COOK TIME: **20 MIN**   4 SERVINGS (ABOUT 16 MEATBALLS)

Smart Snacks & Sides

Homemade Hummus with Veggie Sticks

INGREDIENTS:

FOR THE HUMMUS:
1 CAN (15 OZ) CHICKPEAS, RINSED AND DRAINED (OR 1 ½ CUPS COOKED CHICKPEAS)
2 TABLESPOONS TAHINI
2 TABLESPOONS OLIVE OIL
2 TABLESPOONS FRESH LEMON JUICE
1 GARLIC CLOVE
¼ TEASPOON SEA SALT
2–3 TABLESPOONS WATER (TO THIN AS NEEDED)
OPTIONAL: PINCH OF CUMIN OR SMOKED PAPRIKA
FOR DIPPING:
1 CUP CARROT STICKS
1 CUP CUCUMBER STICKS
1 CUP BELL PEPPER STRIPS
1 CUP CELERY STICKS

INSTRUCTIONS:

In a food processor, combine chickpeas, tahini, olive oil, lemon juice, garlic, salt, and optional spices. Blend until smooth.
Add water, one tablespoon at a time, until desired consistency is reached.
Transfer hummus to a bowl and drizzle with a little extra olive oil if desired.
Serve with prepared veggie sticks for dipping.
Clean Eating Tip
Making hummus at home avoids preservatives and lets you control the flavor and texture. Pair with colorful raw vegetables for a nutrient-dense, fiber-rich snack.

 PREP TIME: **10 MIN**

 SERVINGS: **4**

Roasted Chickpeas with Paprika

INGREDIENTS:

1 CAN (15 OZ) CHICKPEAS,
RINSED, DRAINED, AND
PATTED DRY
1 TABLESPOON OLIVE OIL
1 TEASPOON SMOKED
PAPRIKA
½ TEASPOON GARLIC
POWDER
½ TEASPOON SEA SALT
¼ TEASPOON BLACK
PEPPER

INSTRUCTIONS:

Preheat oven to 400°F (200°C). Line a baking sheet with parchment paper.
Spread chickpeas on the sheet and pat dry with a towel (the drier they are, the crispier they'll roast).
Toss chickpeas with olive oil, paprika, garlic powder, salt, and pepper.
Roast for 30–35 minutes, shaking the pan halfway through, until golden and crispy.
Allow to cool slightly before serving. Chickpeas will crisp up more as they cool.
Clean Eating Tip
For the crispiest texture, dry chickpeas thoroughly before roasting and avoid overcrowding the pan. Store leftovers in an airtight container at room temperature to maintain crunch.

 PREP TIME: **10 MIN**   COOK TIME: **35 MIN**   SERVINGS: **4**

Apple Slices with Almond Butter

INGREDIENTS:

2 CRISP APPLES (SUCH AS
FUJI, HONEYCRISP, OR
GALA), SLICED
4 TABLESPOONS ALMOND
BUTTER (ABOUT 2
TABLESPOONS PER
SERVING)
OPTIONAL TOPPINGS: A
SPRINKLE OF CINNAMON,
CHIA SEEDS, OR CRUSHED
NUTS

INSTRUCTIONS:

Wash and slice apples into wedges.
Arrange on a plate and serve with almond butter for
dipping or spreading.
Add optional toppings for extra flavor and texture.
Clean Eating Tip
Pairing apples with almond butter balances natural
fruit sugars with protein and healthy fats, making this
a satisfying, energy-boosting snack. Choose raw or
unsweetened almond butter for the cleanest option.

 PREP TIME: **10 MIN**   SERVINGS: **2**

Greek Yogurt Ranch Dip with Cucumber

INGREDIENTS:

FOR THE DIP:
1 CUP PLAIN GREEK YOGURT
1 TEASPOON DRIED DILL (OR 1
TABLESPOON FRESH DILL,
CHOPPED)
½ TEASPOON GARLIC POWDER
½ TEASPOON ONION POWDER
1 TEASPOON FRESH LEMON
JUICE
¼ TEASPOON SEA SALT
¼ TEASPOON BLACK PEPPER
FOR DIPPING:
2 CUCUMBERS, SLICED INTO
STICKS OR ROUNDS

INSTRUCTIONS:

In a small bowl, whisk together Greek yogurt, dill,
garlic powder, onion powder, lemon juice, salt,
and pepper until smooth.
Slice cucumbers into sticks or rounds.
Serve dip chilled with cucumber slices for
dipping.
Clean Eating Tip
Using Greek yogurt instead of sour cream keeps
this dip high in protein and low in fat. Pair with
cucumbers—or other raw veggies—for a
refreshing, nutrient-dense snack.

 PREP TIME: **10 MIN**

 SERVINGS: **4**

Chicken Quinoa Bowl *Recipe*

INGREDIENTS:

FOR THE GUACAMOLE:
2 RIPE AVOCADOS
1 SMALL TOMATO, FINELY DICED
¼ SMALL RED ONION, FINELY DICED
1 GARLIC CLOVE, MINCED
1 TABLESPOON FRESH LIME JUICE
2 TABLESPOONS FRESH CILANTRO,
CHOPPED (OPTIONAL)
¼ TEASPOON SEA SALT
¼ TEASPOON BLACK PEPPER
FOR DIPPING:
2 CUPS CARROT STICKS

INSTRUCTIONS:

Scoop avocados into a bowl and mash until mostly smooth, leaving some chunks if desired.
Stir in tomato, onion, garlic, lime juice, cilantro (if using), salt, and pepper. Mix well.
Serve guacamole immediately with carrot sticks for dipping.
Clean Eating Tip
Swap chips for carrots (or other crunchy veggies like bell peppers and cucumber) to keep this snack fiber-rich, low in refined carbs, and nutrient-dense.

 PREP TIME: **10 MIN**

 SERVINGS: **4**

Trail Mix with Nuts & Seeds (no added sugar)

INGREDIENTS:

½ CUP RAW ALMONDS
½ CUP RAW WALNUTS
¼ CUP PUMPKIN SEEDS (PEPITAS)
¼ CUP SUNFLOWER SEEDS
¼ CUP UNSWEETENED COCONUT
FLAKES (OPTIONAL)
¼ CUP RAISINS OR
UNSWEETENED DRIED
CRANBERRIES
2 TABLESPOONS CHIA SEEDS OR
FLAXSEEDS

INSTRUCTIONS:

Combine all ingredients in a medium bowl and mix well.
Store in an airtight container at room temperature for up to
1 week.
Portion into small jars or snack bags for grab-and-go
convenience.
Clean Eating Tip
Choose raw or dry-roasted nuts and seeds without added
oils or salt for the cleanest version. Dried fruit should be
unsweetened and free of added sugar or preservatives.

 PREP TIME: **10 MIN**

 4 SERVINGS
(ABOUT 2
CUPS
TOTAL)

Roasted Sweet Potato Wedges

INGREDIENTS:

2 MEDIUM SWEET POTATOES,
SCRUBBED AND CUT INTO WEDGES
1 TABLESPOON OLIVE OIL
1 TEASPOON SMOKED PAPRIKA (OR
REGULAR PAPRIKA)
½ TEASPOON GARLIC POWDER
½ TEASPOON SEA SALT
¼ TEASPOON BLACK PEPPER
OPTIONAL GARNISH: FRESH
PARSLEY OR CILANTRO

INSTRUCTIONS:

Preheat oven to 425°F (220°C). Line a baking sheet with
parchment paper.
Toss sweet potato wedges with olive oil, paprika, garlic
powder, salt, and pepper until evenly coated.
Spread wedges in a single layer on the baking sheet.
Roast for 25–30 minutes, flipping halfway, until golden and
crispy on the edges.
Garnish with fresh herbs if desired and serve warm.
Clean Eating Tip
Sweet potatoes are rich in fiber, beta-carotene, and slow-
digesting carbs. Roasting instead of frying keeps this dish
light and nutrient-packed, perfect as a side or snack.

 PREP TIME: **10 MIN**   COOK TIME: **25 MIN**   SERVINGS: **2**

Cauliflower Buffalo Bites

INGREDIENTS:

1 SMALL HEAD CAULIFLOWER,
CUT INTO BITE-SIZED FLORETS
2 TABLESPOONS OLIVE OIL
2 TABLESPOONS HOT SAUCE
(SUCH AS FRANK'S REDHOT)
1 TEASPOON SMOKED
PAPRIKA
½ TEASPOON GARLIC
POWDER
¼ TEASPOON SEA SALT
OPTIONAL: FRESH PARSLEY
FOR GARNISH

INSTRUCTIONS:

Preheat oven to 425°F (220°C) and line a baking sheet
with parchment paper.
Toss cauliflower florets with olive oil, smoked paprika,
garlic powder, and salt until evenly coated.
Spread florets in a single layer on the baking sheet and
roast for 20 minutes.
Remove from oven, toss with hot sauce, and return to
oven for another 5–10 minutes until tender and slightly
crispy.
Garnish with fresh parsley if desired and serve warm.
Clean Eating Tip
Roasting cauliflower keeps it crispy without frying, and
using a simple hot sauce adds flavor without excess
sugar or additives. These bites make a perfect plant-
based snack or appetizer.

 PREP TIME: **10 MIN**   COOK TIME: **30 MIN**   2–3 SERVINGS

Rice Cakes with Peanut Butter & Banana

INGREDIENTS:

2 PLAIN RICE CAKES
2 TABLESPOONS NATURAL
PEANUT BUTTER (1
TABLESPOON PER RICE CAKE)
1 MEDIUM BANANA, SLICED
OPTIONAL TOPPINGS:
CINNAMON, CHIA SEEDS, OR
UNSWEETENED SHREDDED
COCONUT

INSTRUCTIONS:

Spread peanut butter evenly over each rice cake.
Top with banana slices.
Sprinkle optional toppings if desired and serve
immediately.
Clean Eating Tip
Using natural peanut butter keeps added sugars and
oils to a minimum. This snack provides a balance of
carbohydrates, protein, and healthy fats for
sustained energy.

 PREP TIME: **10 MIN**   SERVINGS: **2**

Naturally
Sweet Treats

62

Dark Chocolate-Dipped Strawberries

INGREDIENTS:

12 FRESH STRAWBERRIES,
WASHED AND DRIED
½ CUP DARK CHOCOLATE
CHIPS (70% CACAO OR
HIGHER)
OPTIONAL TOPPINGS:
CRUSHED NUTS,
UNSWEETENED COCONUT, OR
A LIGHT SPRINKLE OF SEA SALT

INSTRUCTIONS:

Line a baking sheet with parchment paper.
Melt dark chocolate in a microwave-safe bowl in 20-30 second intervals, stirring between each, until smooth.
Dip each strawberry into the melted chocolate, allowing excess to drip off, and place on the prepared baking sheet.
Sprinkle optional toppings over the chocolate while still soft.
Refrigerate for 10–15 minutes, or until chocolate sets.
Serve chilled.
Clean Eating Tip
Choose dark chocolate with at least 70% cacao to maximize antioxidants and minimize added sugar. These make a naturally sweet, satisfying treat that's perfect for dessert or an indulgent snack.

 PREP TIME: **10 MIN**   COOK TIME: 5 **MIN**   4 SERVINGS (ABOUT 12 STRAWBERRIES)

Energy Bites with Dates & Oats

INGREDIENTS:

1 CUP PITTED DATES
½ CUP ROLLED OATS
¼ CUP ALMOND BUTTER OR
PEANUT BUTTER
2 TABLESPOONS
UNSWEETENED SHREDDED
COCONUT (OPTIONAL)
1 TEASPOON VANILLA EXTRACT
¼ TEASPOON SEA SALT
OPTIONAL ADD-INS: CHIA
SEEDS, FLAXSEEDS, CACAO
NIBS, OR DARK CHOCOLATE
CHIPS

INSTRUCTIONS:

In a food processor, pulse dates until they form a
sticky paste.
Add oats, almond butter, coconut, vanilla, salt, and
any optional add-ins. Pulse until well combined.
Roll mixture into 12 bite-sized balls.
Store in an airtight container in the refrigerator for up
to 1 week.
Clean Eating Tip
These energy bites provide natural sweetness from
dates and healthy fats from nut butter, making them a
nutrient-dense, portable snack for pre- or post-
workout fuel.

 PREP TIME: **10 MIN**

 SERVINGS:12
BITES

Baked Cinnamon Apples

INGREDIENTS:

2 MEDIUM APPLES, CORED
AND SLICED
1 TEASPOON GROUND
CINNAMON
1 TEASPOON MAPLE SYRUP
OR HONEY (OPTIONAL)
1 TEASPOON COCONUT OIL
OR OLIVE OIL
OPTIONAL TOPPINGS:
CHOPPED NUTS, RAISINS, OR
A DOLLOP OF GREEK
YOGURT

INSTRUCTIONS:

Preheat oven to 350°F (175°C). Lightly grease a baking
dish with coconut or olive oil.
Place apple slices in the dish. Drizzle with oil and maple
syrup, then sprinkle with cinnamon. Toss to coat evenly.
Bake for 25 minutes, stirring halfway, until apples are
tender and slightly caramelized.
Serve warm, optionally topped with nuts, raisins, or
Greek yogurt.
Clean Eating Tip
Choose naturally sweet apples and limit added
sweeteners for a fiber-rich, antioxidant-packed dessert
that satisfies sweet cravings without processed sugars.

 PREP TIME: **10 MIN**   COOK TIME: **25 MIN**   SERVINGS: **2**

Coconut Chia Energy Bars

INGREDIENTS:

1 CUP ROLLED OATS
½ CUP UNSWEETENED
SHREDDED COCONUT
3 TABLESPOONS CHIA SEEDS
½ CUP ALMOND BUTTER OR
PEANUT BUTTER
¼ CUP HONEY OR MAPLE
SYRUP
1 TEASPOON VANILLA
EXTRACT
OPTIONAL ADD-INS: CACAO
NIBS, DRIED FRUIT, OR
CHOPPED NUTS

INSTRUCTIONS:

Line an 8×8-inch baking dish with parchment paper.
In a large bowl, combine oats, coconut, chia seeds, and any optional add-ins.
In a small saucepan over low heat, warm almond butter and honey (or maple syrup) until smooth. Stir in vanilla extract.
Pour the warm mixture over the dry ingredients and mix until fully combined.
Press mixture firmly into the prepared baking dish.
Refrigerate for at least 1 hour until firm.
Cut into 8 bars and store in an airtight container in the refrigerator for up to 1 week.
Clean Eating Tip
These bars are a great portable snack with healthy fats, fiber, and natural sweetness. Adjust add-ins to boost protein, antioxidants, or flavor without adding refined sugar.

 PREP TIME: **10 MIN**

 SERVINGS: **2**

Almond Flour Chocolate Chip Cookies

INGREDIENTS:

2 CUPS ALMOND FLOUR
½ TEASPOON BAKING SODA
¼ TEASPOON SEA SALT
¼ CUP COCONUT OIL, MELTED
(OR UNSALTED BUTTER)
¼ CUP HONEY OR MAPLE
SYRUP
1 TEASPOON VANILLA
EXTRACT
½ CUP DARK CHOCOLATE
CHIPS (70% CACAO OR
HIGHER)

INSTRUCTIONS:

Preheat oven to 350°F (175°C) and line a baking sheet with parchment paper.
In a medium bowl, combine almond flour, baking soda, and salt.
In a separate bowl, mix melted coconut oil, honey, and vanilla extract.
Combine wet and dry ingredients, then fold in chocolate chips.
Scoop dough into 12 portions and place on the baking sheet, flattening slightly.
Bake for 12–15 minutes until lightly golden. Let cool before serving.
Clean Eating Tip
Almond flour keeps these cookies gluten-free and adds healthy fats and protein. Use dark chocolate with minimal sugar for a healthier indulgence.

 PREP TIME: **10 MIN**   COOK TIME: **15 MIN**   SERVINGS: 12 COOKIES

Frozen Yogurt Bark with Fruit

INGREDIENTS:

1 CUP PLAIN GREEK YOGURT
1–2 TEASPOONS HONEY OR
MAPLE SYRUP (OPTIONAL)
½ TEASPOON VANILLA EXTRACT
½ CUP MIXED BERRIES
(STRAWBERRIES, BLUEBERRIES,
RASPBERRIES), CHOPPED IF
LARGE
2 TABLESPOONS
UNSWEETENED SHREDDED
COCONUT OR CHOPPED NUTS
(OPTIONAL)

INSTRUCTIONS:

Line a baking sheet with parchment paper.
In a bowl, mix Greek yogurt, honey (if using), and vanilla extract until
smooth.
Spread yogurt mixture evenly over the parchment-lined baking sheet,
about ¼–½ inch thick.
Sprinkle with berries and optional toppings. Gently press into the
yogurt.
Freeze for 2–3 hours, or until completely firm.
Break into pieces and serve immediately, or store in an airtight
container in the freezer.
Clean Eating Tip
This frozen treat is naturally sweetened with fruit and provides protein
from Greek yogurt. Perfect for a guilt-free dessert or an energizing
snack on hot days.

 PREP TIME: **10 MIN**    FREEZE TIME: 2–3 HOURS   SERVINGS: **4**

Oatmeal Raisin Energy Cookies

INGREDIENTS:

1 CUP ROLLED OATS
½ CUP ALMOND FLOUR
¼ CUP NATURAL ALMOND
BUTTER OR PEANUT BUTTER
¼ CUP HONEY OR MAPLE
SYRUP
1 TEASPOON VANILLA EXTRACT
½ TEASPOON CINNAMON
¼ TEASPOON SEA SALT
¼ TEASPOON BAKING SODA
½ CUP RAISINS
OPTIONAL: 2 TABLESPOONS
CHIA SEEDS OR FLAXSEEDS

INSTRUCTIONS:

Preheat oven to 350°F (175°C) and line a baking sheet with
parchment paper.
In a large bowl, combine oats, almond flour, cinnamon, salt,
and baking soda.
In a separate bowl, mix almond butter, honey, and vanilla
extract until smooth.
Combine wet and dry ingredients, then fold in raisins and
optional seeds.
Scoop dough into 12 portions and place on the baking sheet,
flattening slightly.
Bake for 12–15 minutes until lightly golden. Let cool before
serving.
Clean Eating Tip
These cookies are naturally sweetened with honey and raisins
and provide sustained energy from oats and healthy fats.
Perfect for a pre- or post-workout snack.

 PREP TIME: **10 MIN**   COOK TIME: **25 MIN**   SERVINGS:
12 COOKIES

Peanut Butter Stuffed Dates

INGREDIENTS:

8–10 MEDJOOL DATES,
PITTED
¼ CUP NATURAL PEANUT
BUTTER
OPTIONAL TOPPINGS:
CRUSHED NUTS,
UNSWEETENED COCONUT,
OR A PINCH OF CINNAMON

INSTRUCTIONS:

Slice each date lengthwise, creating a pocket, and remove
the pit if not already pitted.
Fill each date with about ½ teaspoon of peanut butter.
Sprinkle optional toppings over the stuffed dates if desired.
Serve immediately or store in an airtight container in the
refrigerator for up to 3 days.
Clean Eating Tip
This snack combines natural sweetness from dates with
protein and healthy fats from peanut butter, making it a quick
energy-boosting treat without added sugars.

 PREP TIME: **10 MIN**

 4 SERVINGS
(8–10
DATES)

Thank You

To everyone who has welcomed one of my cookbooks into your kitchen — thank you. Whether you've flipped through for inspiration, cooked your way from cover to cover, or simply enjoyed one cozy breakfast or hearty dinner along the way, I'm deeply grateful.

Each book I create is a reflection of the meals that bring people together — meals made with love, shared with laughter, and remembered long after the dishes are done. Knowing that these recipes may be part of your mornings, celebrations, or everyday moments is the greatest reward.

If you've enjoyed cooking from any of my books, I'd be so thankful if you took a moment to leave a kind rating or short review. Your words help others discover these recipes and keep me inspired to continue sharing new ones. Thank you for being part of this journey, for cooking with heart, and for making space at your table for my work.
With heartfelt gratitude,

Printed in Dunstable, United Kingdom